A CENTURY
OF RUSSIAN SONG

A Century of

Russian Song

from

GLINKA *to* RACHMANINOFF

Fifty Songs

Collected and edited by

KURT SCHINDLER

Being Vol. XVI of the Golden Treasury of Music

NEW YORK
G. SCHIRMER

A Century of Russian Song

This collection of fifty Russian songs, ranging from old-master Glinka well nigh a century ago to present-day composers like Glazunoff and Rachmaninoff, is the first comprehensive anthology of its kind outside Russia, and means the opening of an almost entirely new repertoire for the English and American concert-hall and drawing-room The collector of these songs hopes that those who read these direct and sincere utterances of a great nation may derive from them a pleasure equalling the delight which he himself has experienced during the years spent in collecting and selecting them. He also ventures to hope that others will follow his initiative, inasmuch as these songs are indeed a key to the understanding of Russia's great symphonic music, so familiar to our concert audiences, and to everything that is national and based on folk-lore

About my leading principle in the selection of the songs, I want to state, that I have not tried to find the most beautiful ones—a very vague definition, regarding which every man would decide differently—nor the ones that I personally like best (in fact, the limitation of space excluded some of the well-known and still beautiful Rubinstein and Tschaikowsky favorites, that are already available in separate editions);—but I chose those songs that seemed to bring the most characteristic message to the world, that are the most direct expression of the Russian national character.

Until about ten years ago Russian music had been identified chiefly with Tschaikowsky's music Besides Glinka's operas, which were intermittently taken up in non-Russian opera houses, and Rubinstein's music, which arose and to a great extent vanished with the brilliant meteoric career of this virtuoso-genius, no Russian music came into prominence on the international market before Tschaikowsky, yet it was not the national element in him, not his operas and ballets, and early symphonies deeply rooted in racial feeling, that appealed to foreign nations, but it was the later Tschaikowsky, the polished, cosmopolitan, aristocratic musician, that captivated everywhere Strongly perfumed, highly seasoned music, which dazzled and agitated the senses, appealed to the emotions, and seemed a particularly characteristic expression of our modern nervous times (before R. Strauss offset it, of course)

Symphonic conductors who were in touch and sympathy with Russian music persevered

here and there in introducing works by Balakirew Rimsky-Korsakoff, Glazunoff, some con-
cert singers included in their repertoire romances by Cui, Borodine, Arensky — yet it re-
mained for the discriminating musicians and the sympathetic understanding of the public of
Paris in the past five years to discover that Russia's greatest musician, the greatest musical
individuality this Slavic nation has possessed, Modest Petrovitch Moussorgsky, had lived
and died in misery some twenty-five years ago, unknown to the outer world, yet leaving a
marvellous bequest to his nation and to the world —compositions so strikingly new and orig-
inal that they seem to rank ahead of the most modern living composers, and which it would
take generations thoroughly to absorb and appreciate. Claude Debussy and Alfred Bruneau
have testified to his glory. Raoul Pugno has enlisted his noble enthusiasm in his cause, and a
Russian admirer of his, Mme Olénine d'Alheim, has given years of self-sacrificing effort to
propagating Moussorgsky's music by lecture-recitals in France and Belgium and by books
and pamphlets, with the result that nowadays scarcely a song-recital in Paris or London is
given without some of Moussorgsky's music, and that New York is fast following on the
trail. The lavish production of his opera "Boris Godounow" in Paris in 1908 by Serge de
Dnaghileff and Gabriel Astruc, with Th. Chaliapine in the title-rôle, has meant a complete
victory for his genius, and most of the European opera houses have included this work of
almost Shakespearian breadth and tragedy in their repertoires.

When Sergei Rachmaninoff toured America in 1909-10 as a pianist, this occasion was
seized by a few singers to introduce his songs. He, of all living Russian composers, seemed
the one most truly gifted in the domain of song. The spirit of the Russian landscape, its
delicate fragrance, its vast and melancholy immensity, speak from the pages we have col-
lected.

Glinka, the founder of Russian art-music, who with single-handed effort wakened the dor-
mant elements of Russian folk-lore, elevating them to an artistic standard, and who at once
established the national Russian school with all its characteristics of rhythm, harmony, and
instrumentation, is represented by celebrated arias from his two best-known operas, music
that is closely related to the contemporaneous German music of Weber and Marschner, but
which nevertheless speaks its own idiom distinctly and forcibly.

Glinka's and Dargomijsky's ballads represent the period of romanticism in Russian music,
they are elegiac, despairing, sentimental, they were written to move hearers to tears, and they
did so unfailingly. Wonderful is the atmosphere of the Russian salons of 1840-50 that these
are.

A Century of Russian Song

ballads exhale: young men with romantic, lofty ideas: hypersensitive, *schwärmerische* ladies, desperate passions and infinite longing. All the *milieu* of Eugene Onegin, of which Pushkin and Tschaikowsky sang — It is strange to see how the styles of Beethoven and Schubert become amalgamated with Russian melodic strains, and with what appealing results, as in Dargomijsky's Elegy (on a Moonlight-Sonata accompaniment), or in his "Prisoner in Siberia," who apostrophizes the "heavenly clouds" that are banished and homeless like himself

Among the many songs of Rubinstein that would have been worthy to enter this collection, we felt it most important to call the attention of singers and public again to his "Persian Songs," those strange exotic blossoms, full of the sensuous charm and vivid imagination of the Arabian Nights, that he, being of oriental descent, was able to give posterity These songs are so graceful and dainty, and so beautifully written for the voice, that the world is bound to take them up again

Borodine, though born earlier than Tschaikowsky, Cui, and Balakirew, represents more fully the ultra-modern type of musical Russia He was never a professional musician and his music always breathes the spirit of aristocratic leisure, refined surroundings, and cultivated city life. Songs like the iridescent "Sea Queen," the strange-scented 'Flowers of Love, the mysterious "Sleeping Princess," the short and poignant "Dissonance," show a marvellous sense for coloristic effects, which he produced by an harmonic scheme very similar to what is now called "Debussyism," but a method that he invented and practised long before Debussy

In his "Song of the Dark Forest" Borodine has gone back to melodic and rhythmic traditions of early mediæval Russian music (as preserved in some of Russia's old wend folksongs), the effect of a bard reciting a ballad being brought out with stirring and overpowering force.

Many songs of Cui and Balakirew might have been included, but their message did not seem so important or characteristic, nothing that the other composers had not better expressed or more strongly, so the former is represented only by the deliciously humorous 'Poet and Critic" disguised as Cuckoo and Nightingale the latter by his song "Oh, come to me," most popular in Russia, but little known elsewhere, a melody of such sweet charm, that no one having heard it can escape its haunting loveliness

More than one-half of this book is devoted to the music of Moussorgsky, Tschaikowsky, and Rimsky-Korsakoff fitly termed Russia's three greatest song-writers

Of the younger generation that followed them, none has yet reached the heights attained by them. Arensky, well known by his piano-compositions, never rises beyond a certain salon-atmosphere in his songs. Glazunoff has given his best in symphonic compositions of rather characteristic tendencies. Their two songs here included, 'Little Fish's Song' and 'Nereid,' are respectively characteristic in their limpid charm and graceful melodious contours.

Among Tschaikowsky's well-known songs it was a question of selecting some hidden beauties that seem worthy of becoming universal property. How charming is the sketch called 'Evening,' that evokes the picture of Little Russian hillsides so irresistibly, such a sweet, fragrant country picture, that is in music what Gogol's landscape-descriptions in his novels are to poetry. His weird oriental "Canary-Song" evokes the exotic splendors, the palms and mosques of the far-off east and the simple folk-tune like "Legend," so poignant and appealing, more simple than Massenet's complicated "Legend of the Sage-brush," and that setting of Tolstoy, "At the Ball," which has moved and will continue to move audiences to tears.

Rimsky-Korsakoff, the prolific opera-composer and gentle-hearted old wizard, who lived long enough to see his fame spread over the entire world, and who was feasted like a king of music when he came to Paris a year before his death (1908), was more fortunate than his comrade and bosom-friend Moussorgsky. These two composers made common cause in seeking and systematically gathering the treasures of Russian folk-song. But while Rimsky-Korsakoff shaped his music after the pattern of folk-song in a somewhat philistine, school-masterly way, Moussorgsky, who went into the subject heart and soul was so imbued and identified with the national expression, that his songs seem almost the emanations of the entire race standing behind him.

Of Rimsky we give three early songs (1866-67), the "Southern Night," the weird "He-brew Love-Song" and the melancholy 'Georgian Hills,' which are much in the same class as Borodine's songs, and three airs from his highly colored fairy opera "Snegourotchka (Little Snowflake), full of innocent charm and dainty rhythms.

I should have liked to give all Moussorgsky's work, but in the choice of eleven songs I hope to have shown him in his most characteristic aspect. Two cradle-songs of his are like two gems in this selection. Not being content with a rocking, lilting accompaniment and a sweet floating melody, he draws the interior of a peasant's hut, the mother with infinite tenderness bending over her child dreaming of its future. he makes us hear the tr'.

mother's sigh, the infant's breathing, the ticking of the large clock, we feel the loneliness of it all Marvellous pictures these two, of which the "Peasant Cradle-Song" must have been particularly dear to the composer, since he inscribed it to the memory of his mother Here he finds for the angelic vision at the end harmonies of purple and gold, and draws melodies of mediæval Byzantine outlines

Martha's song, from his last opera, "Khovanstchina," is an original folk-song, which he frames from verse to verse in a new and richer accompaniment The "Divination by Water" from the same work is an extremely powerful composition, the opening "Invocation of the Spirits" being of almost ghastly and hypnotic effect And now the vast loneliness, the desperate banishment of Siberia looms up from the throbbing of the downcast and muttered final phrases.

There is much sadness, much melancholy in Moussorgsky's music, as there is in all Russian poets and book-writers—Turgenieff, Dostojewsky, Tolstoy, just as any great art, being sincere, must mirror the true state of a nation But in all art, I know of little that can be compared to Moussorgsky's "By the Water," from his song-cycle ' Where no Sun Shines," in its mysterious fatality, its "Hamletian" meditation over the deepest riddle of life It is not surprising that this composer, who in his music was wont to knock at the very gates of death, should have adopted the inspiration of his poet-friend Count Golenitchew-Koutouzow to write a cycle of Death-dances according to the conception of Holbein Of these four song-paintings we present "Death and the Peasant" (Trepak), written on the weird rhythms of the Russian peasant-dance Strange is the Epilogue to this song, which makes us realize the majestic indifference of nature to the misery of the individual The poor peasant lies frozen under the snow, but the sun shines again, spring comes into the land, changing the rigid ice-fields to laughing rivulets and pools, and the merry lark soars to heavenly heights, singing its pæan of happiness.

A different peasant-dance is the "Hopak," which irresistibly draws us into its whirl, and makes us acquainted with a savage Russian sister of Carmen. "The Siege of Kazan," a ballad inserted in the opera "Boris Godounow," gives us a wild picture of mediæval Cossack-life, surely inspired by Gogol's master-novel, "Taras Bulba" The "Oriental Chant," which figures in his short Joshua-Cantata as a middle movement for solo contralto, is a strain that he caught from the lips of the Jewish peasant-people, most characteristic in its wailing and plaintive melody.

88784

A Century of Russian Song

Not the least important among the wide and diverse fields of Moussorgsky's compositions are his nursery-songs, of which we quote that dainty little sketch called 'Child's Song," comparing a child to a blossom, and "The Beetle," telling of a child who, playing in the garden, comes face to face with the problem of a beetle's death

A fitting *envoi* to this collection is Rachmaninoff's setting of Tolstoy's "Billowy Harvest-field' May the golden grains of these Russian sheaves fall into fertile soil, and be reaped in a manifold harvest.

In order to facilitate the recital of these songs in English-speaking countries, especial care has been bestowed by Mr Henry G Chapman and others on the translations, which not only cover the poetical idea of the originals, but also closely follow the trend of the music Fifty new songs, of undoubted value, should afford ample opportunity to promote the introduction of standard music in the English language. There is every reason that English-speaking countries should take up these songs in their own language instead of in exotic translations

KURT SCHINDLER

May 30, 1911

Index of Composers

ARENSKY, ANTON STEPANOVITCH   PAGE

Little Fish's Song   *(Freckless Lied)*   High   212

BALAKIREW, MILY ALEXEJEVITCH

"Oh, come to me !"   (*" Viens près de moi !"*)   High   155

BORODINE, ALEXANDER PORPHYRJEVITCH

A Dissonance   High (or Medium)   68

Flowers of Love   *(Fleurs d'Amour)*   Medium   62

Sea Queen, The   *(La Reine de la Mer.)*   High   64

Sleeping Princess, The   Medium   70

"Slowly the daylight departs"   (« *Lentement baissa le jour* »)   From the opera "*Prince Igor* "
High (or Medium)   76

Song of the Dark Forest   *(Chanson de la Forêt Sombre.)*   Medium   58

CUI, CÉSAR ANTONOVITCH

Poet and Critic   *(Nachtigall und Kukuk)*   Medium   84

DARGOMIJSKY, ALEXANDER SERGIEVITCH

Heavenly clouds   Medium (or Low)   21

Only I ove !   *(Nur lieben !)*   Medium   30

" Ye dear fleeting hours "   *(,, Ihr flüchtigen Stunden".)*   High (or Medium)   26

GLAZUNOFF, ALEXANDER

Nereid, The.   High   220

GLINKA, MICHAIL IVANOVITCH

"Ah kindly star "   *(,, Du trauter Stern")*   From the opera "*Russlan and Ludmilla* "   High   3

"How sweet it is, when I'm with you "   *(,, Wie süss ist's, kann bei Dir ich sein)*   High (or Medium)   10

"The truth is suspected."   *(,, Sie ahnen die Wahrheit")*   Aria of Soussanine, from the opera
"*A Life for the Czar*'   Baritone   16

MOUSSORGSKY, MODEST PETROVITCH

Beetle, The   High (or Medium)   92

By the Water   Medium   102

Child's Song   *(Chanson d Enfant)*   High (or Medium)   100

Cradle-Song of the Poor   *(La Berceuse du Pauvre)*   Medium   132

Death and the Peasant   (*La Mort et le Paysan*)   Trepak   High (or Medium)   116
Divination by Water   (*La Divination par l'eau*)   From the opera "*Khovanstchina*"   Low   108
Hopak   High (or Medium)   136
Martha's Song   (*Chant de Marthe*)   From the opera "*Khovanstchina*")   Medium (or Low)   126
Oriental Chant   Lamentation from the cantata "*Josua Navine*"   Medium   152
Peasant Cradle-Song   (*Berceuse du Paysan*)   From the drama "*Voyevoda*"   Medium   87
Siege of Kazan, The   From the opera "*Boris Godounove*"   Baritone   144

RACHMANINOFF, SERGEI VASSILIEVITCH

"Before my window"   High   228
"How sweet the place!"   Medium   232
Islaes   High   226
Morning   Medium (or Low)   229
"O thou billowy harvest-field!"   High (or Medium)   235

RIMSKY-KORSAKOW, NICOLAS ANDREJEVITCH

A Southern Night   (*Nuit méridionale*)   Medium   202
Hebrew Love-Song   (*Chanson hébraïque*)   Medium   190
Little Snowflake's Arietta   From the fairy opera "*Snegourotchka*"   High   187
On the Georgian Hills   (*Sur les collines de Georgie*)   High (or Medium)   193
Song of the Shepherd Lehl   From the fairy opera "*Snegourotchka*"   High (or Medium)   196
Sylvan Roundelay   From the fairy opera "*Snegourotchka*"   High   206

RUBINSTEIN, ANTON

"Bend, lovely bud"   (,,*Neig', schöne Knospe*")   High   54
"Be not so coy, my pretty maid"   (,*Thu' nicht so sprode, schones Kind*")   High   33
"I feel thy breath blow round me"   (,,*Ich fühle deinen Odem*")   High   52
"My heart all beauty takes from thee"   (,,*Mein Herz schmuckt sich mit dir*")   High   48
"Not with angels"   (,,*Nicht mit Engeln*")   High   42
"When I see those little feet of thine"   (,,*Seh' ich deine kleinen Fusschen an*")   High   38

TSCHAIKOWSKY, PETER ILJITCH

At the Ball   (*Inmitten des Balles*)   High   164
A Legend   (*Legende*)   Medium   168
Canary, The   (*Le Canari*)   High   182
Evening   (*Le Soir*)   High (or Medium)   178
Springtime   (*Frühling*)   High (or Medium)   160
"Tis evening"   From the opera "*Pique Dame*"   Duet for Soprano and Alto   172

Index of Titles

		PAGE
A Dissonance (High or Medium)	A BORODINE	68
Ah, kindly star (High)	M I GLINKA	3
A Legend (Medium)	P TSCHAIKOWSKI	168
A Southern Night (Medium)	N RIMSKY-KORSAKOW	202
At the Ball (High)	P. TSCHAIKOWSKI	164
Beetle, The (High or Medium)	M MOUSSORGSKI	92
Before My Window (High)	S RACHMANINOFF	223
Bend, lovely bud (High)	A RUBINSTEIN	54
Be not so coy, my pretty maid (High)	A RUBINSTEIN	88
By the Water (Medium)	M MOUSSORGSKI	102
Canary, The (High)	P TSCHAIKOWSKI	182
Child's Song (High or Medium)	M MOUSSORGSKI	100
Cradle-Song of the Poor (Medium)	M MOUSSORGSKI	132
Death and the Peasant (High or Medium)	M MOUSSORGSKI	116
Divination by Water (Low)	M. MOUSSORGSKI	108
Evening (High or Medium)	P TSCHAIKOWSKI	178
Flowers of Love (Medium)	A BORODINE	62
Heavenly Clouds (Medium or Low)	A S DARGOMIJSKI	21
Hebrew Love-Song (Medium)	N RIMSKY-KORSAKOW	190
Hopak (High or Medium)	M MOUSSORGSKY	136
How sweet it is (High or Medium)	M I GLINKA	10
How sweet the place! (Medium)	S RACHMANINOFF	232
I feel thy breath blow round me (High)	A RUBINSTEIN	52
Lilacs (High)	S RACHMANINOFF	226
Little Fish's Song, The (High)	A ARENSKY	212
Little Snowflake's Arietta (High)	N. RIMSKY-KORSAKOW	187
Martha's Song (Medium or Low)	M MOUSSORGSKI	126
Morning (Medium or Low)	S RACHMANINOFF	229
My heart all beauty takes from thee (High)	A RUBINSTEIN	48
Nereid, The (High)	A GLAZUNOFF	220
Not with angels (High)	A RUBINSTEIN	42

Index of Titles (continued)

		PAGE
Oh come to me! (High)	M BALAKIREW	155
Only love! (Medium)	A S DARGOMIJSKY	30
On the Georgian Hills (Medium)	N RIMSKY-KORSAKOW	193
Oriental Chant (Medium)	M MOUSSORGSKY	152
O thou billowy harvest-field! (High or Medium)	S RACHMANINOFF	235
Peasant Cradle-Song (Medium)	M MOUSSORGSKY	87
Poet and Critic (Medium)	C A CUI	84
Sea Queen, The (High)	A BORODINE	64
Siege of Kazan The (Baritone)	M MOUSSORGSKY	144
Sleeping Princess The (Medium)	A BORODINE	70
Slowly the daylight departs (High)	A BORODINE	76
Song of the Dark Forest (Medium)	A BORODINE	58
Song of the Shepherd Lehl (High or Medium)	N RIMSKY-KORSAKOW	196
Springtime (High or Medium)	P TSCHAIKOWSKY	160
Sylvan Roundelay (High)	N RIMSKY-KORSAKOW	206
The truth is suspected (Baritone)	M I GLINKA	16
'Tis Evening (Duet)	P TSCHAIKOWSKY	172
When I see those little feet of thine (High)	A RUBINSTEIN	38
Ye dear, fleeting hours (High or Medium)	A S DARGOMIJSKY	26

Index of First Lines

		PAGE
Ah come, weary one	A Borodine	64
Ah! how it hurts!	N Rimsky-Korsakow	187
Ah, kindly star	M I Glinka	3
Ah, stay with me	A Arensky	212
And by day and by night I fare	M Moussorgsky	126
Before my window	S Rachmaninoff	223
Bend, lovely bud	A Rubinstein	54
Be not so coy my pretty maid	A Rubinstein	33
By-bye, by-bye, sleep, my pretty boy	M Moussorgsky	87
By-bye, lower than the humble wayside flower	M Moussorgsky	132
Child Jesus in his garden	P Tschaikowski	168
Cloudlets, ye heav'nly clouds	A S Dargomijsky	21
For to go and gather berries	N Rimsky-Korsakow	206
Hear ye Amorea's daughters	M Moussorgsky	132
Hi! Ha! Ha! The Hopak!	M Moussorgsky	136
How sweet it is when I'm with you	M I Glinka	10
How sweet the place!	S Rachmaninoff	232
Hush! hush! with lovely eyes	A Borodine	70
I feel thy breath blow round me	A Rubinstein	52
I know not how lovely your face is	P Tschaikowsky	164
I love thee, dear!	S Rachmaninoff	229
In the vale, oh! in the valley	M Moussorgsky	100
I sleep	N Rimsky-Korsakow	190
Morning skies are aglow	S Rachmaninoff	226
My heart all beauty takes from thee	A Rubinstein	48
Not with angels	A Rubinstein	42
Now melts the snow	P Tschaikowsky	160
Nursie, listen to what happened	M Moussorgsky	92
O'er yon mountainous height	N Rimsky-Korsakow	202
Oh, come to me	M Balakirew	155
Oh, I love thee so madly	A S Dargomijsky	30

(xvii)

		PAGE
On lovely Touris' shore	A Glazunoff	220
O thou billowy harvest-field!	S Rachmaninoff	235
Pale is the moon	M Moussorgsky	102
Slowly the daylight departs	A Borodine	76
Snowfields in silence	M Moussorgsky	116
Spirits of nether worlds	M Moussorgsky	108
The light of day is slowly fading	P Tschaikowsky	178
The mists are hanging low	N Rimsky-Korsakow	193
The truth is suspected	M I Glinka	16
Thro' the forest's moan	A Borodine	58
Thus Zuleika spoke to her canary	P Tschaikowsky	182
Thy lips say, "I love thee"	A Borodine	68
'Tis evening	P Tschaikowsky	172
To the thunder called the flying cloud	N Rimsky-Korsakow	196
When I see those little feet of thine	A Rubinstein	38
When I stopped at Kazan	M. Moussorgsky	144
When woods are dark	C A Cui	84
Where tears of my passion have fallen	A Borodine	62
Ye dear, fleeting hours	A S Dargomijsky	26

A CENTURY
OF RUSSIAN SONG

"Ah, kindly star"

„Du trauter Stern"

Cavatine from the opera 'Russlan and Ludmilla"

(after Pushkin)

English version by
Henry G Chapman

Michail Ivanovitch Glinka
(1804 - 1852)

mis - tress waits, And all___ her heart is filled with
Freun - din wacht, Ihr Sin - nen nur von dir er -

con passione

mf

thee!___ For thee I long!___ come back to me!___ On thee my thoughts___
füllt!___ Ich har - re dein! o kehr zu - rück!___ ich den - ke dein

pp

___ for ev - er___ dwell,___ My___ hope is all in thee! For thee I
___ zu al - len___ Stun - den, bei dir ist all mein Glück. Ich har - re

p

long! come back to me! On thee my thoughts for ev - er
dein! o kehr zu - rück! ich den - ke dein zu je - der

32723

6

8

in — thine arms I found pro - tec - tion, When I — for - sook — my
dei - nen Ar - men fand — ich Frie - den, als ich ver - liess — das

fa - ther's home, Ah, what to me is life with - out thee? Be-
Va - ter - haus; das Le - ben, ach! was ist's hie - nie - den, ge-

con forza

lov - ed Rat - mir, wilt not come? Come back to me! Come back to
lieb - ter Rat - mir, oh - ne dich! O kehr zu - rück! o kehr zu-

me! Ah, what is life to me with - -
rück! das Le - ben, ach! was ist's hie - -

22724

"How sweet it is when I'm with you!"
„Wie süss ist's, kann bei Dir ich sein"

English version by
Henry G. Chapman

Michaïl Ivanovitch Glinka
(1804-1857)

Allegro moderato

dolciss.

Voice

How sweet it is
Wie süss ist's, kann

Piano

p

p

when I'm with you And si - lent - ly lose ev-'ry feel - - ing Deep,
bei Dir ich sein und still die Ge - dan - ken ver-sen - - ken in's

deep in your eyes____ so blue! The joy of the
Blau' Dei - ner Au - - gen recht tief. Die Lei - den der

22724

heart, and its pain, Will oft in the eyes find ex-pres-sion When
See - le, die Gluth, sie dru - cken sich aus in dem Au-ge, wie's

words might be spok-en in vain, My heart al - ways
Wort es doch nim-mer-mehr thut. Mein Herz es er -

a piacere

trem-bles in si - lenceWhen I am with you!
be - bet im Stil - len, so - bald ich Dich seh'!

colla voce   *a tempo*   *pp*

p

12

How dear is the sight of your face, I watch for your smile with e - mo - - - tion, You seem to em - bod - - y all grace; No aid or as - sis - tance I'd lend To love and its

Dein An - blick, wie lieb ist er mir, ich se - he Dein Lä - cheln mit Won - - ne und An - - muth ver - kör - - pert in Dir. Nicht möch - te ich lei - sten Ge - währ dem Dran - ge der

22724

A Life for the Czar
(1836)

Aria of Soussanine
"The truth is suspected"

Words by Baron Rosen
English version by
Henry G. Chapman

Michaïl Ivanovitch Glinka
(1804-1857)

17

p cantabile spianato ed espressivo

When the_ day shall_ break a - gain, 'Twill be_ the last_ time_ I Shall_ see the sun on high, For death a - waits_ me then! O_ God, when a - go - ny, When tor-ture threat-ens_ me, Have

Bricht du_ an, o_ Mor - gen-roth, dann seh'_ zum letz - ten Mal ich_ dei - nen hol - den Strahl, dann war - tet mein_ der Tod! O_ Gott! in all der Qual die mir die Mar - ter_ droht, er -

22724

18

y! My need is great, Be near, O God, to_ com - fort me! Thro'pain that

Leid! Mein Weh ist gross! Halt, Herr, mir dei - nen Trost be - reit, und stär - ke

now must come ere long, Keep Thou me strong! Oh pit - y, com-fort me,

mich in all der Noth, die bald mir droht! Ja, stär - ke, stär - ke mich

and _ make _ me _ strong! Forsake me not, O God!

in _ mei - ner Noth! Ver-lass mich nicht, o Gott!

Heavenly Clouds

(M Lermontoff)

English version by
Henry G Chapman
and Vera Johnston

A Dargomijsky

On - ward ye has - - - ten, For ban - ished you are, like

me; Driv'n from your dear northern home, To the south _____ ye

come! Tell me, who ban - - - ished

you? Or fate _____ is it fate ye _ fear?

"Ye dear, fleeting hours"

„Ihr flüchtigen Stunden"

Elegie
(D. Davúidoff)

English version by
Henry G.Chapman

German words by Bruno

Alexander Sergievitch Dargomijsky

high beat my heart ___ for joy in my breast! for joy in my breast! Now
hob sich vor Won - ne und Freu-de die Brust, vor Won - ne die Brust! Nun

speech-less and still in-to dark - ness I stare, ___ No star lights my way, My
star - re ich stumm in's Dun - kel hin-ab, ___ kein Stern-lein er-hellt, er-

heart lies in sor-row! No star lights my way, No star sends a ray To
hel - let, er-hel-let, kein Stern - lein er-hellt, kein Stern-lein er - hellt, er -

light-en my way, My heart lies in sor-row, No star lights my
hellt mei-nen Pfad, nur Thrä-nen al-lein sind's, nur Thrä - - nen al-

way,— My heart lies in sor - - row, my heart lies in
lein,— und mein Herz ist so trau - - rig, so trau - - rig, so

sor - - row!
trau - - rig matt!

Only Love!

Nur lieben!

Song

(D. Davuidoff)

English version by
Henry G Chapman

Alexander Sergievitch Dargomijsky
(1856)

Allegretto

Oh, I love thee so, mad-ly,
Wie ich lie - be dich, glu-hend

wild - ly, dear, And to thee a - lone___ is my heart's de - sire, That is
heiss und wild, all' mein Seh-nen ist___ stets nur dir ge-weiht, und doch

ne'er ap - peased, so I greatly fear, That for ver - y pain I may
wird es nim - mer in mir ge-stillt, und ich muss ver-gehn, ach in

well ex-pire! All my
Schmerz und Leid Sieh' mich

a tempo

peace is gone, since my sad mis-chance, Tho' thou be not near, still I
gram-er-füllt, oh-ne Ruh' und Glück, im-mer den-kend dein, ob auch

think of thee, Just a lit-tle word, just a sin-gle glance From thy
fer-ne dir Drum nur ei-nen Gruss, ach, nur ei-nen Blick aus dem

ten-der eyes_ sweet-ly send to me, Just a sin-gle glance, just a
sanf-ten Aug'_ sen-de freundlich mir, ach nur ei-nen Blick, ach, nur

rall

22724

risoluto

sin - gle glance!
ei - nen Blick!

Tho' this
Die - se

a tempo

f

love of mine___ so dis - as - trous be, That its cru - el pain soon my
Lieb' zu dir,___ ach, so schmerzen - reich, weiht er - bar - men - los bald dem

f

death must prove, Yet, O dear-est child, Saint in pu - ri - ty, Yet I
To - de mich. Und doch, sü - sses Kind, hold und en - gel-gleich, kann nicht

dim.   *p*

hate thee not, I can on - ly love, I can on - ly love!
has - sen, nein, kann nur lie - ben dich, kann nur lie - ben dich!

rall.

rall.

f

23734

"Be not so coy, my pretty maid"
„Thu' nicht so spröde, schönes Kind"
(Mirza-Schaffy)

English version by
Henry G Chapman

German words by F Bodenstedt

Anton Rubinstein Op 34, No 11

34

sin - gle, fur - tive kiss_ im - plore,_____
heim - lich ei - nen Kuss_ er - fleh',

one sin - gle, fur - tive
und heim - lich ei - nen

kiss_ im - plore
Kuss_ er - fleh'.

I, who such
Der du so_

22731

36

just for a kiss__ or touch__ of__ hands.
für ei - nen Kuss__ und Hän - - de - druck.

Now ev - 'ry__ kiss I take from
Es wird ein__ je - der Kuss von

thee__ In sing - - ing songs my lips shall use,
dir_____ ein klin - - gend Lied in mei - nem Mund,

22724

And when I press thy hands 'twill be ____ But for an -
und je - der Han - de - druck giebt mir ____ zu ei - nem

oth - er kiss ____ ex - cuse, ____
neu - en Kus - se Grund,

but for an - oth - er kiss ____ ex -
zu ei - nem neu - en Kus - se ____

cuse
Grund

"When I see those little feet of thine"

„Seh' ich deine kleinen Füsschen an"

(Mirza - Schaffy)

German words by F. Bodenstedt
English version by
Henry G. Chapman

Anton Rubinstein. Op. 34, № 3

Voice

Con moto

Piano

mf

When I see those lit - tle feet of thine,
Seh' ich dei - ne klei - nen Füss - chen an,

I can scarce be - lieve, my pret - ty maid - en,   That so much of beau - ty
so be - greif' ich nicht, mein sü - sses Mäd - chen,   wie sie so viel Schön - heit

p

they can car - ry,   So much, so much   beau - ty.
tra - gen kön - nen,   so viel, so viel   Schön - heit;

22724

When I see those slen-der hands of thine, I can scarce be-lieve, my
Seh ich dei-ne klei-nen Hand-chen an, so be-greif' ich nicht, du

pret-ty maid-en,— That— such cru-el blows they can de-liv-er,—
su-sses Madchen,— wie— sie sol-che Wun-den schla-gen kon-nen,—

Cru-el blows can— de-liv-er When I see those ros-y
sol-che, sol-che— Wun-den, Seh' ich dei-ne ros'-gen

lips of thine, I can scarce be-lieve, my pret-ty maid-en,—
Lip-pen an, so be-greif' ich nicht, du su-sses Mad-chen,—

22724

How one lit-tle kiss they can re-fuse me,— How re-fuse one___ kiss.
wie__ sie ei-nen Kuss ver-sa-gen kön-nen, ei-nen Kuss, ei-nen Kuss.

When I see those know-ing eyes of thine, I can scarce be-lieve, my
Seh' ich dei-ne klu-gen Au-gen an, so be-greif' ich nicht, du

pret-ty maid-en,— How for still more love they should be ask-ing
sü-sses Mäd-chen,— wie sie nach mehr Lie-be fra-gen kön-nen;

Than I give thee: Ah, be kind to me!
als ich füh-le. Sieh' mich gnä-dig an!

"Not with angels"

„Nicht mit Engeln"

(Mirza - Schaffy)

German words by F. Bodenstedt
English version by
Henry G. Chapman

Anton Rubinstein. Op. 34, No 1

Not with an - gels in heav-en's vault so blue, Not with ros - es
Nicht mit En - geln im blau-en Him-mels-zelt, nicht mit Ro - sen

in flow - 'ry meads that grew, Not with th'e - ter -
im duf - ti - gen Blu - men - feld, selbst mit der e -

Allegretto

Andante

For an an-gel's heart___ is love-less and for-lorn,___ On the rose___ grows
Denn der En-gel Bu - - sen ist lie-be-leer,___ un-ter Ro - sen___

___man-y a dan-grous thorn, And the sun at night
___dro-hen die Dor-nen her, und die Son - ne___

for - gets to shine,— and the sun—at night,— at night for-gets to
—ver-hüllt des Nachts ihr Licht,— und die Son - ne— ver-hüllt des Nachts ihr

shine, They none— com - pare—
Licht, sie al - - le glei - -

with Zu - lei - - - - ka
- - chen Zu - lei - - - - kha

mine
nicht

Allegretto

Andante

Naught the eye can see____ in the world a - round,____ To lik - en to my____
Nichts____ fin - den,____ so weit das Welt - all reicht,____ die Bli - - cke,____

.... Zu - lei - ka can e'er be found; Sweet,____ thorn - less,____
....was mei - ner Zu - lei - kha gleicht, schön,____ dorn - los,____

22721

and full of love-light rare, sweet,_ thorn - less,_ and full of love - light
voll ew'-gem Lie - bes - schein, schon, dorn - los,_ voll ew'-gem Lie - bes-

rare,
schein,

There's naught_ but her - self_
kann sie_ mit sich selbst_

doth with her_ com-
nur ver - gli - - - - - chen

pare
sein

"My heart all beauty takes from thee"

„Mein Herz schmückt sich mit dir"

(Mirza-Schaffy)

German words by F. Bodenstedt
English version by
Henry G. Chapman

Anton Rubinstein. Op. 34, № 2

Con moto

Piano

mf

sf

My
Mein

p

heart all beau-ty takes from thee, As heav - en from the sun its light, My
Herz schmückt sich mit dir, wie sich der Him - mel mit der Son - ne schmückt, mein

heart all beau-ty takes from thee, As heav - en from the sun its
Herz schmückt sich mit dir, wie sich der Him - mel mit der Son - ne

22724

light.   Thou   art   its   glo-ry,   and____ 'twould be   Lost,____ but for
schmuckt; du   giebst ihm Glanz,   und   oh-ne   dich   bleibt____ es   in

thee, in end-less night, Thou   art its glo-ry   and____ 'twould be   Lost, but for
dunk-le Nacht ent-ruckt, du   giebst ihm Glanz,   und   oh-ne   dich   bleibt   es   in

thee,   in   end-less   night ____   Ah! ____
dunk-le Nacht ent-ruckt ____   Ah! ____

____   Ah! ____
____   Ah! ____

while, And on-ly all her grace_____ re-veals, When once a-
fliesst, und nur, wenn ihr die Son - - ne lacht zeigt, was sie

gain her sun will smile, And on-ly all her grace_____ re-veals, When once a-
Scho-nes in sich schliesst, und nur, wenn ihr die Son - - ne lacht, zeigt, was sie

gain her sun will smile _____ Ah!_____
Scho - nes in sich schliesst _____ Ah!_____

_____ Ah!_____
_____ Ah!_____

dim.

p

"I feel thy breath blow round me"

„Ich fühle deinen Odem"

(Mirza-Schaffy)

German words by F. Bodenstedt
English version by
Henry G. Chapman

Anton Rubinstein. Op. 34, № 6

I feel thy breath blow round me
Ich füh-le dei-nen O-dem

Wher-ev-er I may be,
mich ü-ber-all um-weh'n,

Wher-e'er my eyes may wan-der
wo-hin die Au-gen schweifen,

Thy face I seem to see.
wähn' ich dein Bild zu seh'n.

And in the sea of my spir-it
Im Mee-re mei-ner Ge-dan-ken

The thought of thee ne'er dies,
kannst du nur un - ter - geh'n,

But like the sun at morn-ing
um wie die Son - ne Mor-gens

In beau-ty to a - rise.
schon wie-der auf - zu - steh'n

Ah!
Ah!

Ah!
Ah!

Ah!
Ah!

Ah!
Ah!

Ah!
Ah!

Ah!
Ah!

22724

"Bend, lovely bud"
„Neig', schöne Knospe"
(Mirza-Schaffy)

English version by
Henry G. Chapman
German words by F. Bodenstedt

Anton Rubinstein. Op. 34, No 8

Allegro

Piano

for _____ I _____ would love _____ thee _ and
ich _____ will ____ dich pfle - - gen und

hold _____ thee.
hal - - - - - - ten.

rit.

a tempo

Thou in _____ my arms shalt warm _____
Du sollst _____ bei mir er - war - -

thee, And here _____
men, und sollst _____

22724

Song of the Dark Forest

Chanson de la Forêt Sombre

English version by
Henry G Chapman
French version by
M D Calvocoressi

A Borodine
(1568)

Thro' the for - est's_ moan, thro' the for - est's_ sigh,
La fo - rêt fré - mit, la fo - rêt qui_ bruit

runs a song 'Tis an an - cient tale, sung of days gone by,
chante un chant Un chant d'au - tre_fois, un très vieux ré - cit,

59

stead - i - ly, And this might - y folk grew more pow - er - ful, Now in
s'ac-croissant, Et le peu - ple fort de - ve - nait plus grand, Et ven -

ven - geance they fell on the cit - y folk, and they
geurs puis - sants, ils ont pris la ci - té, ils y

slaugh-tered them, and their en - e - mies did they laugh to scorn, and they
sont en - trés et les en - ne - mis, ils les ont rail - lés, ils se

steep'd them-selves in the blood that ran cursed flood!
sont gri-sés de leur sang mau-dit, à grands flots!

Free-dom, lib-er-ty! Peo-ple
Li-bres, li-bre-ment, peu-ple,

great and free!
peu-ple grand!

Flowers of Love

Fleurs d'Amour

English version by
Henry G. Chapman

French words by
Paul Collin

A. Borodine

Where tears of my pas-sion have fall-en, Full
Mes lar-mes d'a-mour ont fait naî-tre des

man-y a flow-er has sprung,
fleurs au par-fum tendre et doux,

And man-y a sigh I have ut-tered The night-in-
Mes tris-tes sou-pirs ont mê-lé leur mur-mu-re aux

Più animato e cresc
gale has sung
chants des oi - seaux
And couldst thou, couldst
Si tu veux m'ai -
— thou but love me,
- mer à ton tour,
For thee, dear, the flow - ers would
mi - gnon - ne, les fleurs sont pour
rall.
spring,
toi,
And un - der thy win - dow for ev - er To
et sous ta fe - nê - tre les doux ros - si -
f
rall
thee would the night - in - gale sing!
gnols chan - te - ront nuit et jour!
p
pp

The Sea-Queen

La Reine de la Mer

English version by
Henry G. Chapman
French words by
C. Grandmougin

A. Borodine
(1868)

Ah come, wear-y one, make haste, it is eve; Thy heart is throb-bing for

Ac-cours, voy-a-geur, ac-cours; c'est la nuit; ton cœur est tout pal-pi-

me,
tant;

Here 'neath the wave
sous l'eau qui fuit

waits my
mon roy -

king - dom for____ thee!
au - - me t'at - - tend!

Come
Viens

hith - er and rest, For
te re - po - ser sous

cool is my breast, And
mon frais bai - ser, glis -

22724

wan - der at will thro' the deep;
sant sur les flots sans ef - fort;

pp

When
Ber -

thee I have kiss'd, Thou't call me blest:
cé dans mes bras tu me bé - ni - ras,

I
je

love thee! All's a - sleep!
t'ai - me! Viens, tout dort.

ppp

Più animato e cresc.

It
Sur

cresc.

22724

Dedicated to Modest P. Moussorgsky

A Dissonance

Romance

English version by
Kurt Schindler

Words and Music by
A. Borodine
(1868)

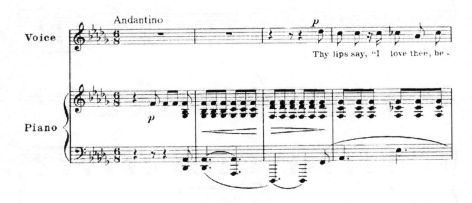

Thy lips say, "I love thee, be -

lieve me;" And yet, in the sound of thy

22225

voice   A false note rings, that doth grieve me,   It

is   in thy smile,   in thine eyes!   Thou know'st,   thou canst not de-

ceive me!

Dedicated to Nicolaj A. Rimsky-Kórsakoff

The Sleeping Princess

Musical Fairy-tale

English version by
Henry G. Chapman

Words and Music by
A. Borodine
(1867)

Doom'd to dream in for-est haunt-ed. Hush! Hush!

Più mosso

Sud - den on the

si - lence break - ing, Laugh-ing, shout-ing, mer - ry - mak - ing,

Thro' the gloom the wood-nymphs sweep, Yet they do not break her sleep

72

Pale and wan, as dead she were, Sleeps the Prin-cess ev - er there

Hush! Hush!

Some do say that on a day A charm-ing Prince, true-

22734

days go by, a - las! Like a dream they seem to

pass, Yet no Prince has ev - er come To in -

vade the for - est's gloom.

Tempo I

Fast a - sleep the Prin - cess lies, Wrapp'd in mys - ter -

y her eyes, By a fair-y charm en-chant-ed, Doom'd to dream in

for-est haunt-ed! Hush! Hush!

Bale-ful charm and slum-ber fell:— Will she wake? Ah, none can

tell!

"Slowly the daylight departs"

«Lentement baissa le jour»

Recitative and Cavatina from the opera
"Prince Igor"

English version by
Henry G. Chapman

Alex. Borodine
1834–1887

Slow - ly the day - light de - parts,
Len - te - ment bais - sa le jour

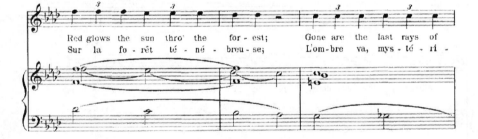

Red glows the sun thro' the for - est; Gone are the last rays of
Sur la fo - rêt té - né - breu - se; L'om - bre va, mys - té - ri -

sun - set, Dark - ness on earth is de - scend - ing; night - la - den
eu - se, É - veil - ler l'é - cho d'a - mour... É - cho di -

shad-ows shroud hill and val-ley In veils of dark-ness.
vres-se, Chant de ten-dres-se, Qui nous ca-res-se!

rall *a tempo* *cresc poco a poco*
Oh balm-y night of the South! What dream of love dost thou
Tiè - de nuit d'a-mour. Ah! Mal-gré l'ar-deur de ta

rall *mf* *ppp cresc poco a poco*

waft us? Thou a-wak'st de-sire in our hearts, to love thou call-est!
flam-me, Tu m'es doux, ô rêve et la foi rem-plit mon â - me!

mf

animato ed appassionato
Wait'st thou for me, O dear-est heart's de-sire?
Chè - re bien-ai - mée, une é-toi-le luit!

fp *mf*

22724

thee! Come to me! O quick-ly come! My
el! Viens, ré - ponds à mon ap - pel! Dou-

rall e dim   *a tempo*

heart,— sweet maid, calls to thee! Know'st thou how— the
ter— d'un cœur est cru - el! Viens!— Ton a -

cresc poco a poco

pain of love— glows in my heart? Warm———— in
mour est— ma vi - e A toi———— tou -

me glows for thee my heart,— sweet love!
jours, tendre a - mie! En - tends— ma voix!

Gladly would I give my life for thee!
Viens, ah viens, é - toi - - le de mon ciel!

Why then tar - riest thou, Love? Haste thee, haste to
Ô ma bien - ai - mé - e, Lais - se - toi flé -

me Come with - out fear, the world is still now,
chir Que crain - dre dans l'ombre em - bau - mé - e?

and sunk - en deep in sleep rests in the
Tout dort en paix, tout dort, sous un ciel

22724

to me! My heart, sweet maid, calls to
A toi ce cœur brû-lant d'a-

thee! O come, the night thy flight shall cov-
mour! La nuit d'é-té, sous ses longs voi-

er, When all save dreams at rest shall be.
les, Pour nous an-non-ce son re-tour.

When hearts with love are brim-ming o-ver,
Il n'est i-ci que les é-toi-les,

And heav'n a - lone   is   there   to   see   The world is
Ces yeux du   ciel   tout pleins d'a - mour   Vois des beaux

still,   and in   night's arms   all
soirs   le doux   sa - phir,   Tout

things   sleep!_____   Oh
va   dor - - mir   Oh

come!_____
viens!_____

22724

Poet and Critic

Nachtigall und Kukuk

(A. S. Pushkin)

English version by
Henry G. Chapman
German words by
L. Esbeer

César Antonovitch Cui. Op. 57, № 22

Andantino ($\quad=72$)

Piano

p

mf

When woods_____ are dark and late the hour,_____
Es singt_____ der Sän - ger dunk - ler Näch - te

A min - - strel lauds_____ the Spring - tide's pow - er;
im Wald_____ das Lob_____ der Früh - lings-mäch - te.

He trills,_____ he war - bles, won - drous bird._____
Er rollt,_____ er tril - lert, pfeift und schlägt.

22734

The cuc - koo then comes forth to bel - low,
Doch ist der Ku - kuk auch zur Stel - le,

The sil - ly, chat - ty, nois - y fel - low, And shouts his "Cuc -
der schwatz-haft al - ber - ne Ge - sel - le, und schreit sein Ku -

- koo," un - de - terred And scur - vi - ly does Ech - o serve us,
- ku un - ent - wegt. Das E - cho weiss den Ruf zu nut - zen

22721

For she re - peats him o'er and o'er, E - ter - nal - ly!
und wie - der - holt ihm im - mer - zu zum Ü - ber-druss!

The Lord pre-serve us From such a
Mag Gott uns schüt - zen vor solch' e -

mel - - - an - chol - y bore!
le - - - gi - schem Ku - - ku.

To the memory of my mother
Julia Ivanovna Moussorgsky

Peasant Cradle-Song

Berceuse du Paysan

English version by
Henry G Chapman
French version by
Hettange

From the drama "Voyevoda," by Ostrowski

Modest Moussorgsky
(1865)

By - bye, by - bye, sleep, my pret-ty boy,
Do - do, do - do, mon bel et beaugas,

Sleep, little one, sleep, thou hum-ble toil-er's babe
Dors, en-fant, dors, en-fant du la-bou-reur

By - bye, by - bye,
Do - do, do - do

In the bright-er days ___ of yore our ___ lot was not so
Dans l'ancien temps, ___ on a-vait moins de ___

hard But now ___ a - las, the happy times are o'er Dis - tress ___ and
mal! Main - te - nant, tout le long des longs jours, le noir ___ sou-

grief And des - pair ___ have we, And there's no ___ re-
ci, ___ les en - nuis ___ cru - els, la mi - sè - re nous

lief from our mi - se - ry.
tra - vail-lent sans ré - plt.

89

the hot sun shall blaze.
dar - de - ra ses feux.

dim.

pp *dolce*

Now, while sleep doth thine eye - lids en - fold,
Le som - meil a fer - mé tes bons yeux.

Thy soul far a way from the earth may
Ta douce âme a pris sa vo - lée au

fly, And yet the_ Lord watch-es ev - er nigh, An-gels o - ver
loin No - tre Sei - gneur veille au-près de toi L'an-ge t'a . cou -

ben suonato   *un poco rit*   *a tempo*

thee spread their wings of gold, spread their wings of gold
vert de son ai - le d'or, de son ai - le d'or.

armonioso   *dim*   *pp*

dim   *ppp*

Dedicated to V. V. Stássoff

The Beetle
Le Hanneton

English version by
Henry G. Chapman

Words and Music by
M. Moussorgsky

No. 5 of the cycle, "Nursery Songs"

blocks of ma-ple, those Moth-er made me,

dar-ling Moth-er, and so nice-ly And my lit-tle

house was fin-ished with the roof on, just like an-y

real one Ah!

22724

A bee - tle light - ed on the roof, So big and black and mon - strous thick. And reached out his feel - ers,

hor - - ri - bly, and stared at me with

glar - - ing eye - balls!

cresc

f *mf*

Oh, how scared I was! The bee - tle

sf *f* *sf*

buzzed fierce - ly, And he spread his

p *cresc*

22794

wings out, and then he tried to grab me____

Then up he flew, and struck me up - on my fore - head!

I held my breath then, Nur - sie, kept still, a -

fraid to move a fin - ger! But out of just one eye I peep'd at

him   And Nur - sie,   O   Nur - sie, think of it!

On his back there lay the bee - tle, ver - y still, with legs all droop-ing,

no   long - er   an - - gry.   And he did not

move his feel - ers,   and was not buzz - - ing,

98

just his wings were wav - ing gen - tly. Was he

cresc.

dead, then? Or just pre - tend - ing?

f

Tell me, how was that? Do tell me, Nur - sie,

f

22724

a - bout this bee - - tle!___ The bee - tle

struck me, but he fell o - - ver!

dim *ritard*

Tell me why he lay there, poor bee - tle!

A Child's Song

Chanson d'Enfant

English version by
Henry G. Chapman
French words by Hettange

(L. Mey)

Modest Moussorgsky

Andantino tranquillo

Voice

Piano

In the vale,— oh! in the val-ley,
Dans le val,— ah! dans le val-lon,

cresc.

Grows a lit-tle ber-ry, Ri-pen'd by the
a pous-sé la mû-re. Le so-leil la

cresc.

sun-ny hours, Glad-den'd by the show-ers.
fait ro-se, L'eau du ciel l'ar-ro-se.

riten.

In the lit - tle cha - let
Dans le clair sa - lon ____

Lives a maid - en mer - ry, Whom her fa - ther spoil - eth,
un en - fant mur - mu - re, Son pa - pa l'a - pai - se,

For whom moth - er toil - - eth
Sa ma - man la bai - - se

By the Water

(Count A. Golenistchew-Koutouzow)

English version by
Kurt Schindler

Modest Moussorgsky
No. 6 of the Cycle:"Where No Sun Shines"

Silent I gaze on the tide, while a - lone a - wake, And in my soul strange fore - bod - ings of fate a - rise

22721

Soft - ly the rip - ples are

flash - ing in sil - v'ry light,

On balm - y breez - es there

trem - bles a ma - gic spell;

Spell - - bound I lis - - ten, en -
thrall'd by an un - known fear, -
If it should bid me stay,
Then could I ne'er de-part; Bade it me

hence, I should fly with a wound - ed heart,

poco rall   *a tempo*

Called it to me, I should plunge in the

wa - ters here!

Divination by Water*

La Divination par l'eau

From the opera "Khovanstchina"

English version by
Kurt Schindler

French version by
Hettange

Modest Moussorgsky
(composed 1875-1881)

Spi - rits of neth - er worlds, Hid - den be - low the floods!
O vous, es - prits des eaux! O vous, es - prits sub - tils!

Bound by a ma - gic spell Deep in the dark and void! Hear! I call ye!
Mâ - nes per - dus au loin dans le noir né - ant, je vous man - de!

er basin filled with

Poor, per-ished hu-man souls! Vic-tims of des - ti - ny! Ye that to mor - tal men
Pau-vres hu-mains noy-és! Tris-tes es-prits dé-chus! Vous qui pou-vez tra-hir

Fate's se-crets can be-tray, Hark to me! Tell me what life will bring
tous les se-crets du sort, ê-tes-vous là? De ce sei-gneur trou-blé,

Un - to the proad Bo - iár, Who in the grasp of fear Dread-eth his fu-ture lot. What
de ce bo-iar fiè-vreux que l'a-ve-nir é-meut, et que la crainte é-treint, quel

22724

fate is his?
est le sort?

Lim-pid the wa-ter and crystal clear,
L'eau est lim-pi-de comme un cris-tal:

Yet 'neath the sur-face I
El-le bra-sil-le de

see mys-te-rious flames.
feux é-tin-ce-lants.

Prince! See the wa-ter-spir-its
Prin-ce! l'es-prit des eaux

Prince! they have barr'd the way to thee,
Prince! ils te bar - rent le che - min,

They sum - mon thee to a long, wear - y jour - ney:
Ils te font voir u - ne rou - te loin - tai - ne.

Now I see! I see! I see clear - ly! Look ye!
Ah! je vois! je vois! tout s'é - clai - re! Prin - ce!

22724

114

vain ____ Were thy sor - row:— This thy fate ev - er -
leur____ vai - ne, c'est____ là ton lot dé - sor -

more! Nay! Naught can a - vert this from
mais! Non! rien ne pour - ra te sau -

thee. Nei - ther chance nor thy will; Thou wilt strive,____ but in
ver, ni ha - sard, ni vou - loir; tes ef - forts____ se - ront

vain, Thy fate is de - creed. O
vains. Le sort l'a vou - lu. Tu

Death and the Peasant
La Mort et le Paysan
Trepak
(Count Golenistchew-Koutousow)

English version by
Kurt Schindler and H.G.Chapman
French words by Hettange

Modest Moussorgsky
(1875)
No. 1 of the Cycle: "Songs and Dances of Death"

Lento assai, tranquillo

Voice

Snow - fields in si - lence.— So cold is the night.
Bois, champs et plai - ne s'al - lon - gent dé - serts.

Piano

And the i - cy north-wind is wail - ing, Bro-ken-ly sob-bing,
La ra - fa - le pleu - re, s'é - ner - ve. On di - rait là - bas,

as though a ghast - ly dirge O - ver the
là - bas, dans la nuit, plain - tes au -

fp dim.

graves it was chant-ing — Lo! O be-hold!
près d'u-ne tom-be .. oui! C'est ce-la!

p poco a poco più mosso

Through the night a strange pair ap-proach-es,
Dans la nuit,— un pauvre hom-me

poco a poco più mosso

Death holds an old peas-ant fast in his clutch-es
La mort l'é-treint, le ca-res- - -se

22724

See, now they dance the tre - pak, do the pair,_____
El - - le l'en - traine a - vec el - - le si loin!_____

pp

poco rall.

Songs at his ear Death is sing - - - - ing:
En lui chan - tant u - ne ron - - - - de:

poco rall.

Allegretto moderato e pesante

"Hey, poor old man with a head so light! Too much you drank on the
O pau - vre vieux, pau - vre vieux sans tê - te! Ah! il a bu, il a

p

f (à 3 battute)

road to - night! And the lash - ing snow-flakes set your head a -
bu en rou - te! Mais le vent, la nei - ge tour - nent, vi - rent,

mf

mf

Ancora più sostenuto

Heap _____ him a
Fais - - - - lui son

(a 5 battute)

bed in your play, wild
lit, ô ma bri - - se

breez - - es! Hey! _____
fol - - le! Et _____

for a dance, for a
dan - se - lui, chan - te -

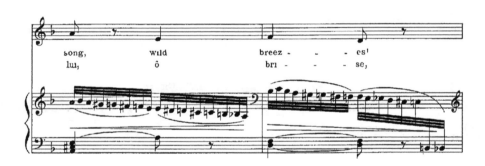

song, wild breez - - es!
lui, ô bri - - se,

Meno allargando, mosso

Sing your songs, ye night - winds, Storm-ing from the
Un jo - li re - frain___ qui l'en - dor - me

Andante tranquillo

Sleep,   friend, in — peace, close your eyes for
Dors,   mon a - mi, dors en paix, sans

ev - er!   Spring   comes, but
crain - te!   Voi - ci ve -

you'll   see it nev - er!
nir   les beaux jours!

Soon the sun   up - on the fields will smile; —
Sur   les   grands sei - gles et les blés —

And   the   peas - ants   come to till   the soil,___
clair   so - leil'   Tout flam - be'

To   the cloud - less   skies___   mer-ry larks a - rise!___
Et   les chants s'é - pan - dent,   re-di-sant la joi - e'

mf *ritard*   *p*   *pp* *a tempo*

a tempo

p ritard   *p*   *pp*

Martha's Song

Chant de Marthe

From the opera "Khovanstchina"

English version by
Henry G Chapman
French version by
Hettange

Andante con moto e lamentoso ($\quad$=96)

Modest Moussorgsky
(composed 1875–1881)

And by day and by night I fare
Et de jour et de nuit je vais

O - ver moun - tain and mead - ow, o - ver moun - tain and
par les champs et les prés____ verts, par les champs et les

meadow, Thro' the woods and o-ver the burn-ing sands

prés_ verts, par les bois et par les ter-rains brû-lés

On the bram-bles I've torn my hands, Worn my feet so they

Aux buis-sons j'ai grif-fé mes mains, J'ai sur le sol u-

scarce will move. Ev-er I seek_ the one I love. Yet I

sé_ mes pieds Tou-jours cher-chant mon bien-ai-mé, je n'ai

find_ not him that is dear_ to me

pas_ re-trou-vé ses traits_ ché-ris.

22724

Once to his palace I dared to go Ah, I crept there so
je m'a-ven-tu-rais vers son pa-lais je me glis-sai fur-

fur-tive-ly! First I rapped at his win-dow, Then I
ti-ve-ment, je heur-tai sa fe-nê-tre, je son-

struck on the sil-ver bell— a blow,
nai du mar-teau dar-gent— tin-tant

Dost not re-mem-ber, my dear____ one? Ah, call to mind all you
Sou-viens-toi, sou-viens-toi, ché - ri! Oh, sou-viens-toi de tes

prom - ised me! Of - ten a - lone in the night I've thought of thy
ser - ments! Seu - le, j'ai son-gé des lon - gues nuits à tes

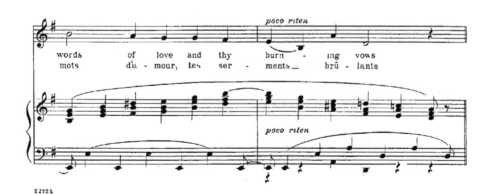

words of love and thy burn - ing vows
mots d'a - mour, tes ser - ments____ brû - lants

Poco meno mosso

mistico

Like   two ta   -   -   pers   of   the   Lord,
Tels   les cier -   ges   du   Sei - gneur

pp

Thou   and   I shall be   flames of light!   E - ven chil - dren of
nous   al - lons tous deux clair - flam - ber!   Fil - les du Christ dans

poco riten.

Christ in ra - diance, Our souls in their fire shall be   lift-ed on   high!
la   lu - miè - re,   et   dans le feu   nos   â - mes   s'é - lè - ve - ront!

poco riten.

Cradle-Song of the Poor

(Berceuse of Yerómushka)*

La Berceuse du pauvre

(Nekrassow)

French Words by Hottinger
English version by
Henry G. Chapman

Modest Moussorgsky

By - bye, by - bye!
Do - do, do - do,

By - bye, by - bye!
do - do, do - do.

Low - er than the hum - ble way-side flow'r
Bas, plus bas que l'humble fleur des champs,

Bowed my I - van's head must be,
il de - vra courber le front,

If this child of low - ly folk____ and poor
mon I - van, l'enfant des pau - vres gens,

* Yerómushka means in Russian: "little Jerome".

134

By - bye, by - bye! By - bye, by - bye!
Do - do, do - do, do - do, do - do.

No - ble court-iers ev-er night and day   To my I - van will pay court,
Les plus no - bles, et soir et___ ma-tin,   te fe-ront ci - vi - li - tés,

La - dies drest in silk and sa - tins gay,
Chez les bel - les da - mes en sa - tin

23734

Hopak

French words by Hettange
English version by
Henry G. Chapman

(Words by L. Mey, after the
Little-Russian of Shevtchénko)

Modest Moussorgsky
(1867)

Allegro
quasi pizzicato

Piano

Hi!   Ha! Ha!
Hoï!   hop! hop!

the   Ho - pak!   I'm   the   wife   of   a   Ko - sak!
au   Ho - pak!   Je   suis   fem - me   d'un   Ko - sak!

Laugh he won't, for he's too crust-y, Red his head, his
Il rit peu,— mais il se ri-de, il est roux jus-

bod-y rust-y. Ah, my fate, my luck-less fate! Yah!
qu'à la rouil-le. Ah! mon sort, mon tris-te sort! Hoï!

Eh, but I'll not
A quoi bon ver-

cry for ev-er, Go, my friend, lap up the riv-er!
ser des lar-mes? Va, mon vieux, à la fon-tai-ne!

La - ter one, and two, and three! When the girl gets up_ to go,_
puis en-core un, deux et trois! Et la femme a - lors s'en va,

She will have a man_ in tow,_ To her jeal - ous
un jeune hom - me sur_ ses pas_ Le ma - ri ja -

hus - band's call_ She will pay no heed at all_
loux l'ap - pel - le, mais il n'a qu'un pied de nez_

Hey, my man, if yours I be, See that you pro-vide for me· Yes, Sir!
Si je suis à toi, mon vieux, tu me dois pour-voir de tout· oui - da!

23724

Get this al - so thro' your head, Chil-dren must be cloth'd and fed! Just so!
Il te faut soi-gner l'en-fant, le nour-rir et le vê-tir: oui, oui!

Now, un-less these things you do, I shall soon get rid of you: Tru-ly!
Ou si-non, é-coute un peu: je me pas-se-rai de toi: oui-da!

Yes, my friend, the ba-by's there, Wash his face and curl his hair! There, now!
Le pe-tit est là, mon vieux: la-ve-le, bi-chon-ne-le: oui, oui!

Just you mind now what I say! Do not try to
Mais vois - tu, prends garde à toi! Ne vas pas quit -

The Siege of Kazan

Varlaám's Ballad

From the opera "Boris Godounow"

(after Púshkin and Karamzín)

English version by
Henry G.Chapman

Modest Moussorgsky
(1872)

Czar for plea-sure tar - - ried,

How the Ta - tars then he har - ried,

How he scourged them with - out pit - y! Let no one

say___ a word!

22724

On that
night by stealth Czar I - van drew his men round Ka - zan; Ring the
town and drive his mines be - low the riv - er, his plan! Proud-ly
strut - ted thro' the cit - y Ta - tars bold from near and far,

"We will send to hell", said they," this ter - ri - ble Czar!" Cru - el

Ta - tars were they!

Then Czar I - van lower'd his lord - ly head,

Gloom - y and dark his face be - came with rage as he said.

"Now, brave can - non - iers, be - gin your game!
Read - y with your fus - es; strike your flame! Can - non -
iers, strike your flame!"

Poco meno mosso (♩ = 126)
From the tin - der the wax - en ta - pers catch the

crash!

sf *poco accel.*

mf

Tempo I

Oh, the Ta-tars rent the air with aw-ful shriek and

mf

cry, Cries of hor-ror, shrieks of

f

mf

men who die! And Czar I - van

mf

f

m.s.

piled them up moun - tains high! Man - y_a

thou-sand leg and arm, hip and thigh! Leg and arm, hip and

thigh! When I

stopped at Ka - zan, that fine old cit - y! Hey!

Oriental Chant
(Lamentation)
From the cantata "Josua Navine"

English version by
Henry G. Chapman

Modest Moussorgsky
Arr. by Kurt Schindler

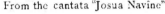

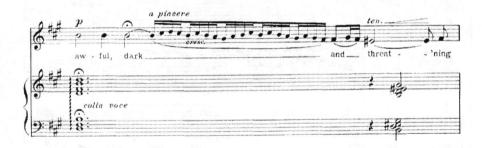

Printed in the U.S.A.

brow! Hear ye A- mo- re- a's daugh- ters, hear their la- men- ta- tion un- to Ca- naan, un- der Ga- jem's aw- ful, dark and threat'ning brow!

'Neath the walls of Ga-va - o - na, Falls the

bro-ken crown of ___ A - mo - re - a, Whence are flow - - ing ___

Streams of bit - - - - ter tears.

Dedicated to Cesar A Cui

"Oh come to me!"

(A Koltsow)

English version by
Alma Strettell

French words by
M D Calvocoressi

«Viens près de moi»

M Balakirew

Oh come to me when breez-es
Viens près de moi, lors-que la

stir The si-lent trees with lan-guid sigh-ing, When field and
brise in-cli-ne mol - le-ment les ar - bres, lors-que le

156

Poco più agitato

sports and storms in young de - sire!___ Oh come to me, for one with
que mon cœur fré - mit d'ex - ta - se! Viens près de moi, ray - ons u -

thee I fain would taste life's keen - est sa - vor, And, crush'd a -
nis! Je veux goû - ter des joies sans bor - nes, je veux, blot -

gainst that fair young breast, Would hold thee close in love for
ti con - tre ton sein, t'ai - mer, t'é - treindre a - vec dé -

ev - er! Ay, crush'd a - gainst that fair young breast, I'd hold thee
li - ces! Je veux, blot - ti con - tre ton sein, t'ai-mer, t'é -

close in love for ev - er!
treindre a - vec dé - li - ces!

Springtime

Frühling

(Pleshtchéyeff)

English version by
Henry G. Chapman

P. Tschaikowsky. Op. 54, No 9
From the cycle, "Songs for Young People"

22724

all the win-ter's storm and stress   For man-y a day will then be
all' die schlimme Win-ter-zeit   ist wie-der-um vor-bei fur

o-ver   Now hearts a-bout one ev-'ry-where With sud-den
lan-ge,   und auch das Herz im Bu-sen drin be-ginnt so

vim be-gin to quiv-er,   As if, for-sooth, all hu-man
un-ge-stum zu schla-gen,   als war' nun al-les Weh da-

ritenuto ad lib

cresc   *riten colla voce*

care_____   With win-ter days were gone for ev-er!   'Tis hope that
hin_____   fur im-mer mit den Win-ter-ta-gen!   Wie Al-les

a tempo

makes all hearts so gay. "'Tis Spring," on ev-'ry face is

sich der Hoff-nung freut „'s ist Früh-ling!" steht in je-dem

writ-ten, And e - ven those are glad to - day, Whom

Bli - cke, ja, der selbst fühlt sich glück-lich heut; dem

fate with naught but grief has smit - ten We all de - light in Spring, O

Leid ver-lieh'n nur vom Ge-schi - cke Doch wie den Lenz auch Je - der

bliss!___ But birds' and chil-dren's mer - ry___ voic - es Show plain e - nough

preist,___ im Vo - gel-zwit-schein, Kin - der - la - chen zeigt deut-lich sich,

22724

just who it is, That Na-ture's wak-ing most re-joic - es,   Show plain e-nough
wem doch zu-meist will-kom-men der Na-tur Er-wa - chen,   zeigt deut-lich sich,

just who it is,   That Na-ture's wak-ing most re-joic - - es.
wem doch zu-meist will-kom-men der Na-tur Er-wa - - chen

At the Ball

Inmitten des Balles

(A. Tolstoi)

English version by
Henry G. Chapman

German words by
Ferdinand Gumbert

P. Tschaikowsky. Op. 38, № 3

I know not how love - ly your face is, For that, when I
In - mit - ten des Bal - les, ohn' Ab - sicht, um - ge - ben von

met you by chance, Was hid in the cloud of_____ your lac - es, As you
lär - men - der Welt, sollt' ich dich er - bli - cken, ein Räth - sel, das

cresc.

And gra-cious your air, yet a - part,　　Your laugh-ter so
hold schwe-bend die schlan-ke Ge - stalt,　　dein La - chen so

frank and dis - arm - ing　　It al-ways will ring in my heart.
hell und so selt - sam　　ist nicht mehr im Her-zen ver - hallt!

At night, when I sit a - lone,　　wear - y,　　There will in the
In nächt-li - chen Stun-den dann,　　ein - sam,　　leg' ich mich er -

espress.

dark-ness ap - pear Two beau-ti - ful eyes that smile kind - ly,　　The
mü - det zur Ruh', dann seh' ich und hö - re dich e - wig,　　und

Poco meno mosso

sweet-est of voic-es I hear. And oft thro' my slum - bers
vor mir wie da - mals steh'st du Und sink' ich vor Mat - tig-keit

your im - age Like some fleet-ing vi - sion will move:
dann in Schlum-mer, wie qua - len die Traum-bil - der mich

Can this then be love, dear, I won - der? Ah yes, I sup - pose it is
Ich weiss es nicht, was mir ge - sche - hen, ich glau - be gar ich lie - be

Tempo I

love!
dich!

A Legend

Légende

(Poem by Pleshtcheyeff
after an English original)

English version by
Henry G Chapman

French words by
Paul Collin

P Tschaikowsky, Op 54, No 5
From the cycle,"Songs for Young People"

Voice

Piano

Moderato

Child Je - sus in his gar - den
L'en - fant Jé - sus dans son jar -

fair   Some sweet red ros - es once had grown,
din   A - vait plan - té de bel - les roses

22724

And all the gar - den dis - ar - ray. "How now shall your____ poor
Et dé - vas - té tout le jar - din. "Pau - vre cou - ron - ne, com -

crown be made? They have not left a flow'r for you!"
ment la fai - re? Les beaux ro - siers n'ont plus de fleurs!"

"The thorns are left," Child Je - sus said,____ "The thorns are left, and
"Mais les é - pi - nes sont res - té - es, ré - pond Jé - sus, ce -

they will do." So of the thorns a crown he
la suf - fit." Puis, en cou - ron - ne les tres -

172

Duet
From the opera "Pique-Dame"
(1890)

English version by
Henry G.Chapman

P. Tschaikowsky

swift-ly fade, for now the sun's last rays are dy - - ing,

swift-ly fade, for now the sun's last rays are dy - - ing,

One pale grey cloud - rift lies a -

One pale grey cloud - rift lies a -

cross the sun-set light, Like streaks of foam up-on some

cross the sun-set light, Like streaks of foam up-on some

22724

dis — tant o-cean ly — — ing.

dis — tant o-cean ly — — ing.

All morn — ing

All morn — ing

has the air been warm   with threating storm,   But   now a cool — er

has the air been warm   with threating storm,   But   now a cool — er

breeze is blow-ing from the moun - tain, And thro' the win-dow
breeze is blow-ing from the moun - tain, And thro' the win-dow

blows the per - fume of the rose, And soft is heard
blows the per - fume of the rose, And soft is heard

the gen-tle plash - ing of the foun - - tain.
the gen-tle plash - ing of the foun - - tain

22724

No nest - - ling___ from its bed need

No nest - - ling___ from___ its bed need

raise its star - tled head, And in the grass_____ a - lone is

raise its star - tled head,___ And in the grass_____ a - lone is

heard the chirp of crick - - - - - et

heard the chirp of crick - - - - - et

Evening

Le Soir

English version by
Kurt Schindler

French words by
Paul Collin

(L. Mey, after the Little-Russian
of Shevtchénko)

P. Tschaikowsky. Op. 27, N° 4
(1875)

22724

low - ly cot-tage wait - ing, His wife pre - pares the sup - per now
dant, à la chau-mie - re, La fem - me ne perd pas son temps

A - round the board deck'd out so
Pour le sou - per de la fa -

neat - ly The house - hold ga - ther in the hall,
mil - le, Dé - jà, la table est tou-te prê - te,

22724

The come-ly daugh - ter waits on all,
La jeu - ne fil - le va ser - vir.

And while the stars are peer-ing sweet-ly, The night-in - gale pours forth his call.
Et la pre-mière é - toi - le bril - le; Le ros-si - gnol chante a ra-vir!...

Then, o'er the mead-ows per-fume-la - den,
Puis, dans la cam-pa - gne mu - et - te,

No sound is heard, how-e'er so slight,
On n'en - tend plus le moin - dre bruit;

And all is si - lent, all is qui-et. Save the night-in -
Tout fait silence et tout s'en - - dort. Seuls le ros-si -

gale ___ he and the maid - en,
gnol et la fil - let - te

They still are sing-ing in the night!
Chan-tent en - co - re dans la nuit!

The Canary

Le Canari

(L. Mey)

English version by
Henry G. Chapman

French words by
Paul Collin

P. Tschaikowsky. Op. 25, № 4

Moderato

Piano

Thus Zu - lei - ka spoke to her ca - na - ry:
Zu - lei - ka di - sait au ca - na - ri:

Copyright, 1911, by G. Schirmer, Inc.
Printed in the U. S. A.

184

songs you sang so sweet - ly. Where will skies be found that are more sun-ny?
chan-sons les plus dou - ces: Sous quels cieux est-il plus de lu - miè-re?

Gar - dens where are cool - er, fresh-er shad-ows? Where wilt find more
Quels jar - dins ont de plus frais om-bra - ges? Où trou-ver des

sweet - ly scent-ed flow - ers? Where wilt find a
fleurs plus em-bau-mé - es? Où rê - ver maî -

mis - tress half so lov - ing? Sing me now the
tres - se plus ai - man - te? Chan - te - moi tes

22724

songs you sang so sweet-ly!" And the bird re-plied to his sul-ta-na
chan-sons les plus dou-ces.» Et l'oi-seau ré-pond à la sul-ta-ne

"Ah! I pray you, do not__ mock my sad-ness,
"Ah! n'in-sul-te pas à__ ma tris-tes-se,

For I fly no more, no__ more I sing now, How, a-mong the har-em's
Je ne vo-le plus ni__ plus ne chan-te; Ton ha-rem a des é-

mourn-ful ech-oes, How can I re-peat my
chos__ trop som-bres Pour re-di-ie mes chan-

22724

joy - ous car-ols? O - da-lisks in in-do-lence may dwell here,
sons joy - eu - ses. L'o - da-lisque y vit dans l'in-do-len - ce,

Nor re - gret the free-dom that they for-feit, But a bird, more
Sans pleu-rer sa li - ber - té per-du - e, Mais l'oi-seau, plus

proud, less vain, less thought-less, Can - not sing when he is made a slave!"
fier et moins fri - vo - le, Pour chan-ter ne veut pas être es - cla - ve!"

Little Snowflake's Arietta*

From the fairy opera "Snegourotchka" (Act I)
(after A Ostróvsky)

English version by
Henry G Chapman

Nicolas Rimsky-Korsakow

Voice

Ah! _____ how it hurts! and oh, _____ how sad my

Piano

pp

cresc

heart is, for heav-y as a moun-tain lies up-on ___ it this

mf dim

poor ___ dear ___ flow-er Lehl _____ so light-ly threw a-way!

p

* The original is one tone higher, in G minor.

Now off to oth-er maidens has he run, Whose laughter and whose lips are warmer than

mine! Ah,_____ here am I in tears,_____ and oh, so lone - ly! for Lehl he has

scorned me and left me a - lone! Ah, dear-est Lehl, I let you go____ where love

is; yes, go to those who will know how_____ to love you! But why must I be al-ways sad_____

22721

at heart_and al-ways cold and i-cy in my pas - sion? O Father Win-ter, thou hast done me

rit   *a tempo*   *p*

wrong!   Dear Mother Spring, be kind and send to   me   one ti - - ny   spark of

burn - ing heat and flame   at which to   melt   this fro - - zen heart of

mine!

Dedicated to Modest P. Moussorgsky

Hebrew Love-Song

Chanson hébraïque

(L. Mey)

English version by
Henry G. Chapman

French words by
J. Sergennois

N. Rimsky-Korsakow. Op. 7

(1867)

sleep;   my   heart at break of   day can __ nev-er __ sleep:
dors;   mon   cœur, au point du   jour, ja- mais ne __ dort...

At   my thresh- -old waits my   love, and calls __ to   me:
A   ma por- -te mon   ai- mé m'ap-pel- -lect   dit:

Lyrics (English / French):

O - pen, my dear— one, rise— for him who lov - eth thee!
Ou - vre, mi - gnon - ne, lè - ve-toi pour ton— a - mi!

Morn - ing breaks,— the moun - tain-peaks are all a - glow,
L'au - be crois - san - te sur— les monts rou - git dé - jà;

From———— the— grass - es,———— from the moss - y trees,
Aux brins d'her - be,———— sur les troncs mous-sus,

Drops of dew like pearls— are hang - ing, And their tears—
Pend en per - les la— ro - sé - e. Et ses pleurs—

of fire, gems of the dawn, Have be-
bril-lants, joy aux du jour, Ont mouil-

ppp

poco string. *p*

dewed my ra - ven locks. Shad-ows of night now
lé mes noirs che-veux. L'om-bre noc - tur - ne

poco string. *pp* *cresc.*

riten. *pp*

has-ten to westward a-way; O - pen thy
rou-le vers le couchant... Ou - vre ta

mf *riten.* *p*

door and come, O fair - est love!
por - te, viens, ô ma beau-té!

pp *ppp*

On the Georgian Hills

Sur les Collines de Géorgie

(A. S. Pushkin)

English version by
Henry G. Chapman

French words by
J. Sergennois

N. Rimsky-Korsakow. Op. 3, No 4
(1866)

The mists are hang-ing low a - bove the Geor-gian hills, The yel - low Ar is roar - - - ing in the dis - tance; My heart or light or sad or

La bru - me pla - ne sur les monts de l'É - ri - van; L'A - ras mu - git sous ma fe - nê - tre... Cœur tris - te, cœur lé - ger, cœur

Copyright, 1911, by G. Schirmer, Inc.
Printed in the U.S.A.

dull'd,_____since hope is gone_____ Still finds in thee its whole ex-
mor - ne et sans tour - ment, Je vis en toi, c'est tout mon

is - tence, In thee, and thee a - lone.
ê - tre... Qui, toi... toi, rien que toi...

Poco meno mosso

In my_____ de - spon - den - cy
En mon_____ a - bat - te - ment

I feel no pain, nor would re - prove thee; If e'er a-
Au - cune, au - cune an - gois - se ex - trê - me. Si de nou-

gain my heart should wake to life in me,— 'Tis that to live it needs must
veau mon cœur é - prou - ve quel-que é - moi,— C'est que pour vi - vre il faut qu'il

love thee.
ai - me.

Song of the Shepherd Lehl*

From the fairy opera "Snégourotchka"

(after A. Ostrovsky)

English version by
Henry G. Chapman

Nicolas Rimsky-Korsakow

Allegretto giocoso (♩ = 108)

Lehl playing the shawm (rozhók)

Piano

Più lento, maestoso

Lehl

To the thun-der call'd the fly-ing cloud, Rum-ble, grum-ble, while I

poco riten.

Tempo I

scat-ter my rain, Spring-time show'rs shall re-fresh the plain, Hap-py

colla parte

* This is the third song of Lehl, from Act III of the opera

Copyright 1912 by G. Schirmer, Inc.

flow'rs once more to life__shall spring, All the girls will go a-ber-ry-ing, All the

poco riten   *a tempo*

lads will fol-low in their train Lehl, my Lehl, my love, my love, my Lehl'(he plays)

poco riten   *a tempo*   *p*

Più lento

Thro'the

woods the girls a - mong the___ trees Far and wide are pick - ing

mf

poco rit.

straw - ber - ries, Dells and glades with songs and laugh - ter re -

poco rit.

Tempo I

sound. All at once one maid - en can't___ be found; All the

pp

oth - ers, weep - ing sad - ly, cry, "She's been eat - en by some

p

32724

do ___ no good, Bet-ter look a bit a-bout __ the __
wood! Lehl, my Lehl, __ my __ love, my love, my Lehl!

(he plays)

Dedicated to Mili A. Balàkireff

A Southern Night

Nuit méridionale

(N. Stchérbine)

English version by
Henry G.Chapman

French words by
J.Sergennois

N. Rimsky- Kórsakow. Op. 3, No. 2

(1866)

O'er yon mountain-ous height
Dans les cieux val-lon-nés

Rides the Queen of the Night, And the
Bril - le l'as-tre chan-geant; L'o - li -

ol - ive in sil - ver is drest; And the sea as it heaves To the
vier s'en - lu - mi - ne d'ar - gent; Dans leur flux obs - ti - né, Cou-rent,

swell of the waves Is a flame with the gems on its breast
mon-tent les flots Pail-le - tés de leurs riches gre-lots

Ah, mi - ra - cu - lous nights! Ah, mys -
Ces pro - di - ges des nuits, Ce mys -

te - ri - ous lights! All my blood, all my heart is a - fire, I have
tè - re et ces feux, Tout en - flam-me mon sang et mon cœur, Les flam-

ga - thered thee flow'rs For our flame - light - ed bow'rs; Tar - ry
beaux sont bril - lants, J'ai cueil - li quel - ques fleurs, Hâ - te -

not, O my Love, my De - sire! Tar - ry
toi vers mes bras a - mou - reux! Hâ - te

not, O my Love, my De - sire!
toi vers mes bras a - mou - reux!

Soon the night will be o'er,
Cet - te nuit va pas - ser,

And the waves call no more 'Neath the pas - sion-less eye of the
Et la va - gue se tait Sous les yeux im - pas - si - bles du

sun, And I feel how a chill All my bo - som doth
jour, Et le froid vient d'en - trer En mon sein in - qui -

fill: Wilt thou guess how I love thee a - lone?
et Sau - ras - tu de - vi - ner mon a - mour?

Air

"Sylvan Roundelay"
From the fairy opera "Snegourotchka" (Prologue)
(after A. Ostróvsky)

English version by
Henry G. Chapman

Nicolas Rimsky-Korsakow
(1880)

Allegretto capriccioso

For to dance the mer-ry round, and one of them, With the cho-rus led by

shep-herd Lehl to fol-low Hi,_____ La-do Lehl!

'Tis this your daugh-ter would pre-

fer, Or_ life_ is_ lit - tle_worth to_ her

28724

Recit.

Ah, let me go! When you re-turn with win - ter

to re - side, With - in these gloom-y woods, at

Adagio

e - ven - tide, I'll sing to you,

Sing you a song the while the storm-winds pipe and play,

The Little Fish's Song

Fischleins Lied

(From Lérmontoff's poem "Mtziri")

English version by
Henry G. Chapman
German words by L. Esbeer

A. Arensky. Op. 27, No 1
(1901)

2273A

I'll call my sis - ters here and we _____ Will
Die Schwe - stern ru - fe ich her - bei, wir

whirl and dance for thee, _____
schwin - gen uns ___ im Tanz,

Till freed thy wear - y spir - it be, And
bis dei - ne mü - de See - le frei, dein

bright once more thy glance. _____
Au - ge vol - ler Glanz. _____

rit. a tempo

p a tempo dim.

22701

216

here,   so   soft   shall   be   thy   bed,_____   So
aus,   dein   Pfühl   ist   ja   so   weich,_____   die

light   thy   cov -   er   -   let;_____   In   sweet -   est
De -   cke   licht   und   klar;_____   schnell flieht   die

dreams   wilt   thou   for -   get   How   fast   the
Zeit   in   mei -   nem   Reich,   du   träumst,   wirst's

cresc.

time   has   sped.
nicht   ge -   wahr.

22724

Dear lad,   I___ will
O, trau - - - ter___ Schatz,

con - - fess   to thee,   I
ich   hehl'   es nicht,   ich

love   thee e - - - - ven
lie - - - - be dich___   so

so _____   As
sehr   wie

28724

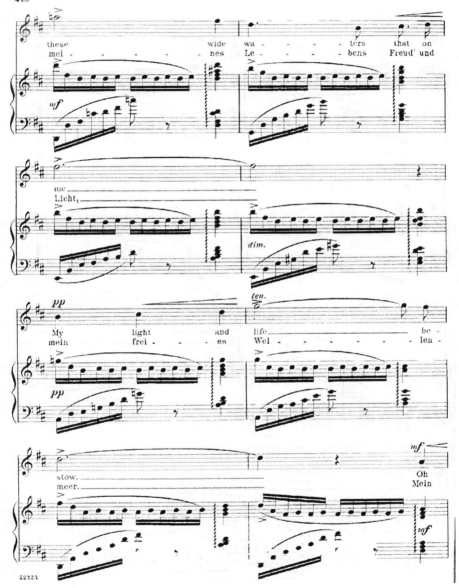

these . . . . . wide wa — — — ters that on
mei — — — — — — — nes Le — — — bens Freud' und

mf

me_____
Licht,_____

dim.

pp   *ten.*

My   light   and   life_____   be-
mein   frei — — es Wel — — — — — len-

pp

stow._____
meer._____

Oh
Mein

mf

mf

love - - - - - ly boy! Oh
trau - - - - - ter Schatz, mein

dear - - - - est lad! Ah,
trau - - - - ter Schatz, o

stay, ah, stay with me!
blei - be hier bei mir!

The Nereid

(A. Pushkin)

English version by
Henry G. Chapman

Alex. Glazunoff. Op. 60, N⁰ 3

Before My Window

(G Galina)

English version by
Henry G. Chapman

Sergei Rachmaninoff Op. 26, No 10

me. And as the scent from frail and trem-bling blos-soms

flies, I catch the in-cense sweet so glad-ly heav'n-ward

soar-ing, I feel a fra-grant breath my sens-es o-ver-

* The higher

pow'r - ing, I hear a song of love,___ ___ that needs no words, a - rise ___

Lilacs

(Kath. Beketoff)

English version by
Henry G. Chapman

Sergei Rachmaninoff. Op.21, No 5

22724

Where it's dew - y and cool,   I must see if my for-tune I'll
das von Tau-trop-fen frisch,   schau' ich, ob dort mein Glück ich nicht

find
find'

Ah,   of luck there's scant dole,   Yet it's ev-'ry-one's
Ja,   des Glücks gibt's nicht viel,   und doch ist's al - ler

Morning

(M L Janoff)

English version by
Henry G Chapman

Sergei Rachmaninoff. Op 4, No 2
(1890)

sun lit up the world with am - 'rous ray, And

with her burn - ing kiss - es smiled and took pos - ses - sion.

The Day,

as tho' he still at heart mis - trust - ed The truth of

22724

aught the dream-y Morn might do or say, Dropped swift-ly

down to earth, and with a smile he dust-ed Au-

ro - ra's my-riad wealth of dia - mond tears a - way

22734

"How sweet the place!"

(G. Galina)

English version by
Henry G. Chapman

Sergei Rachmaninoff
Op. 21, No. 7

lone - - - ly pine, the host of flow'rs,   And

thou, _____ my love - ly dream! _____

"O thou billowy harvest-field!"

(A. Tolstoi)

English version by
Henry G. Chapman

Sergei Rachmaninoff. Op. 4, No 5
(1893)

Nev - er may'st thou be bound in a sin - gle sheaf!

un poco cresc.

Ah, ye thoughts and ye dreams so fraught with care!

Who can gar - ner you in heart or mind!

Who can grasp you or bind you up in words!

O - ver thee, O__ field,_____ hur - ried a

driv - ing storm, Down it bent all thy har-vest of

grain to earth, All_ thy ri-pen'd seed it_ flung a-broad!

Ah, how_ wide-ly_ were ye scat-tered,

O my_ dreams! Yet wher - e'er_

_ one a - mong you has_ fall'n to earth,

There have sprung from the soil weeds of mis - er - y, There has flour-ished the

bit - ter - est heart's dis-tress! Ah!

Ah!   Con moto

Lightning Source UK Ltd.
Milton Keynes UK
UKHW021824300123
416202UK00005B/285